COME SWIFTLY TO YOUR LOVE

Love Poems

of Ancient

Egypt

Translated

by EZRA POUND

and Noel Stock

Illustrated by Tom di Grazia

COME

SWIFTLY

TO YOUR

LOVE

♛ Hallmark Editions

CONTENTS

INTRODUCTION 5

CONVERSATIONS IN COURTSHIP 6

LOVE LYRICS 14

MORE LOVE LYRICS 17

PLEASANT SONGS OF THE SWEETHEART

     WHO MEETS YOU IN THE FIELDS 23

PLEASANT SONGS 30

GARDEN SONGS 32

SWEET PHRASES 37

HASTE 43

INTRODUCTION

These unusual poems are based on literal
renderings of the hieroglyphic texts into Italian
by Boris de Rachewiltz, which first appeared in
the volume *Liriche Amorose degli Antichi Egizioni*
published by Vanni Scheiwiller, Milan, in 1957.
Most of the original Egyptian texts have survived
only in incomplete form, but, for the purpose
of modern adaptation, each poem is presented
as complete. The sources for the poetry are:
the Turin (Maspero) Papyrus, the Harris 500 and
Chester Beatty I & II Papyri in the British Museum,
and the Ostrakon No. 25218 pottery in the Cairo
Museum — all dating between 1567 and 1085 B.C.

CONVERSATIONS IN COURTSHIP

HE SAYS:

Darling, you only, there is no duplicate,
More lovely than all other womanhood,
      luminous, perfect,
A star coming over the sky-line at new year,
      a good year,
Splendid in colours,
      with allure in the eye's turn.
Her lips are enchantment,
      her neck the right length
            and her breasts a marvel;
Her hair lapislazuli in its glitter,
      her arms more splendid than gold.
Her fingers make me see petals,
      the lotus' are like that.
Her flancs are modeled as should be,
      her legs beyond all other beauty.
Noble her walking
            (vera incessu)
My heart would be a slave should she enfold me.

Every neck turns — that is her fault —
      to look at her.
Fortune's who can utterly embrace her;
      he would stand first among all young lovers.

6

Deo mi par esse
    Every eye keeps following her
        even after she has stepped out of range,
A single Goddess,
    uniquely.

SHE SAYS:

His voice unquiets my heart,
    It's the voice's fault if I suffer.
My mother's neighbour!
        But I can't go see him,
    Ought she to enrage me?

MOTHER:

Oh, stop talking about that fellow,
    the mere thought of him is revolting.

SHE:

I am made prisoner 'cause I love him.

MOTHER:

But he's a mere kid with no brains.

SHE:

So am I, I am just like him
and he don't know I want to put my arms round him.
    THAT would make mama talk...

May the Golden Goddess make fate,
    and make him my destiny.

Come to where I can see you.
    My father and mother will then be happy
    Because everyone likes to throw parties for you
        And they would get to doing it too.

SHE SAYS:
I wanted to come out here where it's lovely
    and get some rest,
Now I meet Mehy in his carriage
    with a gang of other young fellows,
        How can I turn back?

Can I walk in front of him
    as if it did not matter?
Oh, the river is the only way to get by
    and I can't walk on the water.

My soul you are all in a muddle.
If I walk in front of him my secret will show,
    I'll blurt out my secrets; say:
                Yours!

And he will mention my name and
     hand me over to just any one of them
       who merely wants a good time.

SHE SAYS:
My heart runs out if I think how I love him,
     I can't just act like anyone else.
It, my heart, is all out of place
     It won't let me choose a dress
       or hide back of my fan.
I can't put on my eye make-up
                  or pick a perfume.

"Don't stop, come into the house."
     That's what my heart said, one time,
And does, every time I think of my beloved.
     Don't play the fool with me, oh heart.
       Why *are* you such an idiot?
Sit quiet! Keep calm
       and he'll come to you.
And my alertness won't let people say:
     This girl is unhinged with love.
When you remember him
     stand firm and solid,
       don't escape me.

HE SAYS:

I adore the gold-gleaming Goddess,
                    Hathor the dominant,
                              and I praise her.

I exalt the Lady of Heaven,
        I give thanks to the Patron.
She hears my invocation
        and has fated me to my lady,
Who has come here, herself, to find me.
        What felicity came in with her!
I rise exultant
        in hilarity
                    and triumph when I have said:
                              Now,
And behold her.
        Look at it!
                    The young fellows fall at her feet.
Love is breathed into them.

I make vows to my Goddess,
        because she has given me this girl for my own.
I have been praying three days,
        calling her name.
For five days she has abandoned me.

I went to his house, and the door was open.
    My beloved was at his ma's side
        with brothers and sisters about him.
Everybody who passes has sympathy for him,
    an excellent boy, none like him,
        a friend of rare quality.

He looked at me when I passed
    and my heart was in jubilee.
If my mother knew what I am thinking
    she would go to him at once.

O Goddess of Golden Light,
        put that thought into her,
           Then I could visit him
And put my arms round him while people were looking
And not weep because of the crowd,
        But would be glad that they knew it
           and that you know me.
What a feast I would make to my Goddess,
        My heart revolts at the thought of exit,
If I could see my darling tonight,
        Dreaming is loveliness.

Yesterday. Seven days and I have not seen her.
My malady increases;
limbs heavy!
I know not myself any more.
High priest is no medicine, exorcism is useless:
a disease beyond recognition.

I said: She will make me live,
her name will rouse me,
Her messages are the life of my heart
coming and going.
My beloved is the best of medicine,
more than all pharmacopoeia.
My health is in her coming,
I shall be cured at the sight of her.
Let her open my eyes
and my limbs are alive again;
Let her speak and my strength returns.
Embracing her will drive out my malady.
Seven days and
she has abandoned me.

Ezra Pound

LOVE LYRICS

I

Diving and swimming with you here
Gives me the chance I've been waiting for:
To show my looks
Before an appreciative eye.

My bathing suit of the best material,
The finest sheer,
Now that it's wet
Notice the transparency,
How it clings.

Let us admit, I find you attractive.
I swim away, but soon I'm back,
Splashing, chattering,
Any excuse at all to join your party.

Look! a redfish flashed through my fingers!
You'll see it better
If you come over here,
Near me.

II

Nothing, nothing can keep me from my love
Standing on the other shore.

Not even old crocodile
There on the sandbank between us
Can keep us apart.

I go in spite of him,
I walk upon the waves,
Her love flows back across the water,
Turning waves to solid earth
For me to walk on.

The river is our Enchanted Sea.

III

To have seen her
To have seen her approaching
Such beauty is
Joy in my heart forever.
Nor time eternal take back
What she has brought to me.

IV

When she welcomes me
Arms open wide
I feel as some traveller returning
From the far land of Punt.

All things change; the mind, the senses,
Into perfume rich and strange.
And when she parts her lips to kiss
My head is light, I am drunk without beer.

V

If I were one of her females
Always in attendance
(Never a step away)
I would be able to admire
The resplendence
Of her body entire.

If I were her laundryman, for a month,
I would be able to wash from her veils
The perfumes that linger.

I would be willing to settle for less
And be her ring, the seal on her finger.

I

Mealtime: time for you to leave?
Your only mistress, I fear, is your belly!

Why hurry? Why shop for clothing
At this hour? Why worry, my love,
The covers on my bed are fine.

You are thirsty?
Here is my breast,
Overflowing.

II

Your love pervades my body
As wine pervades water when
Wine and water mingle.

III

A lotus bud her beauty
Like fruit her breast.

Her face is like a snare in a forest of *meryu*
And I, a poor wild goose,
A poor wild goose drawn down
To take the bait.

IV

Down river to the rhythm of rowers
Going to Memphis, my bundle of rushes
            on my shoulder,
Memphis, known as the "Life of Two Lands."
And to the great god Ptah I will say
"God of Truth, let me lie with my love tonight."

Ah! the very thought turns river to wine,
The wine goes to my head,
Ptah inhabits the river reeds,
Goddess Sekhmet the riverside flowers,
The god Nefertem blooms in the lotus bloom.

The thought of my love's beauty
Is dawn rise
Lighting the sky.

The city of Memphis stands on the skyline
My love's offering

Her chalice of fruit for Ptah
God with the shining face.

V

Damn her, I will go home on sick leave!
And she will be among the neighbours
When they find me.

It will be most interesting to see what she does,
Especially when the doctors arrive and are puzzled.
For she knows more about this illness
Than they do.

VI

My darling's castle has double doors,
Wide open.
Now that she boils with anger
I long to be her doorkeeper
To receive her tongue-lashing.
That way I would be able to hear her
        when she's angry,
Like any young urchin, peeping in terror.

HE

I sail the "King's Waters,"
And then into the waterways of Heliopolis:
My destination the place of tents
At the entrance to Mertu Harbour.
I must hurry!
Restless, excited,
My heart goes out in prayer,
Prayer to the sun god Ra
For a quick, safe voyage.
I will be able to see her
As she walks beside the river.

SHE

With you here at Mertu
Is like being at Heliopolis already.

We return to the tree-filled garden,
My arms full of flowers.

Looking at my reflection in the still pool—
My arms full of flowers—
I see you creeping on tip-toe
To kiss me from behind,
My hair heavy with perfume.

With your arms around me
I feel as if I belong to the Pharaoh.

PLEASANT SONGS OF THE SWEETHEART
WHO MEETS YOU IN THE FIELDS

I

You, mine, my love,
My heart strives to reach the heights of your love.

See, sweet, the bird-trap set with my own hand.

See the birds of Punt,
Perfume a-wing
        Like a shower of myrrh
Descending on Egypt.

Let us watch my handiwork,
The two of us together in the fields.

II

The shrill of the wild goose
Unable to resist
The temptation of my bait.

While I, in a tangle of love,
Unable to break free,
Must watch the bird carry away my nets.

And when my mother returns, loaded with birds,
And finds me empty-handed,
What shall I say?

That I caught no birds?
That I myself was caught in your net?

III

Even when the birds rise
Wave mass on wave mass in great flight
I see nothing, I am blind
Caught up as I am and carried away
Two hearts obedient in their beating
My life caught up with yours
Your beauty the binding.

IV

Without your love, my heart would beat no more;
Without your love, sweet cake seems only salt;
Without your love, sweet "shedeh" turns to bile.

O listen, darling, my heart's life needs your love;
For when you breathe, mine is the heart that beats.

V

With candour I confess my love;
I love you, yes, and wish to love you closer;
As mistress of your house,
Your arm placed over mine.
Alas your eyes are loose.
I tell my heart: "My lord
Has moved away. During
The night moved away
And left me. I am like a tomb."
And I wonder: Is there no sensation
Left, when you come to me?
Nothing at all?

Alas those eyes which lead you astray,
Forever on the loose.
And yet I confess with candour
That no matter where else they roam
If they roam towards me
I enter into life.

26

VI

The swallow sings "Dawn,
        Whither fadeth the dawn?"

So fades my happy night
My love in bed beside me.

Imagine my joy at his whisper:
"I'll never leave you," he said.
"Your hand in mine we'll stroll
In every beautiful path."
Moreover he lets the world know
That I am first among his women
And my heart grieves no longer.

VII

Head out the door—
Is he coming?

Ears alert for his step,
And a heart that never stops talking about him.

A messenger:
"I'm not well..."
Why doesn't he come straight out
And tell me
He's found another girl.

One more heart to suffer.

VIII

I writhe so for lost love
Half my hair has fallen in grief.

I am having my hair recurled and set,
Ready, just in case...

PLEASANT SONGS

I

O flowers of Mekhmekh, give us peace!
For you I will follow my heart's dictation.

When you embrace me
So bright is the light that shines from you
I need balm for my eyes.

Knowing for certain that you love me
I nestle at your side.

My heart is sure that among all
Men you are the main one for me.

The whole world shines
I wish we could go on sleeping together,
Like this, to the end of eternity.

II

So small are the flowers of Seamu
Whoever looks at them feels a giant.

I am first among your loves,
Like a freshly sprinkled garden of grass
and perfumed flowers.

Pleasant is the channel you have dug
In the freshness of the north wind.

Tranquil our paths
When your hand rests on mine in joy.

Your voice gives life, like nectar.

To see you, is more than food or drink.

III

There are flowers of Zait in the garden.
I cut and bind flowers for you,
Making a garland,
And when you get drunk
And lie down to sleep it off,
I am the one who bathes the dust from your feet.

GARDEN SONGS

I

The pomegranate speaks:
My leaves are like your teeth
My fruit like your breasts.
I, the most beautiful of fruits,
Am present in all weathers, all seasons,
As the lover stays forever with the beloved,
Drunk on "shedeh" and wine.

All the trees lose their leaves, all
Trees but the pomegranate.
I alone in all the garden lose not my beauty,
I remain straight.
When my leaves fall,
New leaves are budding.

First among fruits
I demand that my position be acknowledged,
I will not take second place.
And if I receive such an insult again
You will never hear the end of it. . . .

With lotus in bloom
And lotus in bud,
And oil and sweet myrrh of every kind,
You will be among the contented
For the rose pavilion is highly thought of
And well looked after. . . .

There he is!
Let us go up and embrace him
And keep him here all day long.

II

Hear the voice of the figtree:
Compliments to my lady.
Who more noble than I?
Why not I your servant, if you have none?
They brought me from Syria
As plunder for the beloved.

I drink all day, not water
From the water-skin, but beauty.

The little sycamore that you planted
       with your own hands
Moves its mouth to speak.

How lovely his branches, lovely
As they sway, and swaying, whisper,
Their whisper sweet as honey.

The branches bend with plump fruit
Redder than the blood-red Jasper,
Leaves like malachite.

They are drawn to you from afar
Who are not yet in your cool shade.
You entice a love-letter
From the hand of that young girl,
Daughter of the head gardener,
Who runs up to her lover, saying
"Let us go somewhere quiet."

The garden is in full splendour,
With tent pavilions;
And all for you.

My gardeners rejoice to see you.

Send your slaves for the music gear,
Prepare for feasting.

Merely to run towards you is cool water
For a man who is thirsty.

Your servants are coming with beer of every brand,
Cakes, pastries, fresh flowers overflowing
Their baskets, and fresh cool fruit.

Stay one day, one day of happiness,
And tomorrow, and the day after tomorrow,
Three whole days in my shade.

The chosen one sits at his right,
He plies her with liquor
Until she is ready to do anything he says.

With everybody dead drunk,
None of them a clue what is going on,
He pursues his course in earnest.

And that is all I am telling:
My discretion is such
That of the things that follow
I give not a single hint.

SWEET PHRASES

I

My girlfriend's house is rowdy
That is the only way to describe it.
Crammed all night with song and dance
Overflowing with beer and wine.

I consider how melodies entwine,
And finally, after my love has forced the issue
With a request for active cooperation,
I conclude that the night has been worth it,
        after all.

And tomorrow?
The same old song.

II

If you find yourself at the ivy-covered house
Before the other guests arrive,
Make yourself at home
In the banquet hall.

Flowers stir in the breeze,
Which, if it is not smothered by perfume,
Will manage to convey to you
The quality of some of the fragrance, at least.

Perfume spreads,
Drunkenness begins.

That girl there, the one like Noubt:
If you are lucky enough to receive her as a gift,
My friend, you should be prepared
        to offer sacrifice of your life
As the only thing worthy in return.

III

She is a collector of men.

As accurate as the tax-gatherer with his lariat
On the hunt for some poor farmer's cattle.

She fixed me with her eye,
Etherised me with her perfume,
Finally lassoed me with her long dark hair.

And now she has branded me
With her branding-iron of fire.

38

IV

Mouse, why do you whisper love in your heart all day?
Why do you talk about her, incessantly,

All the time, any time
Except when she is present in the flesh?

Damn it all, man
Go to her, and try to look as if you mean business!

V

I find my love fishing
His feet in the shallows.

We have breakfast together
And drink beer.

I offer him the magic of my thighs
He is caught in the spell.

VI

I refuse to put up with her insults.
She made me wait hours at the door when I called

And then when she did come out, she
Didn't even say good evening, the rotten bitch.

God, how she's changed her tune.
She doesn't want to spend the night with me.
She doesn't even want to talk to me.

VII

You arrive at her house,
Your lucky night, perhaps?
I knock and nothing happens.
The doorkeeper must have gone to bed.

Latch! how can I get in?
Please, bolt, wish me luck, be my
Good genie, it's me, your old friend,
I pass this way often.

I promise to offer the following:
        a bull to the interior
        an ox to the latch
        a gazelle to the bolt
        a goose to the catch
If only you will let me in!

Of course the best cuts of meat
Will go to those apprentice carpenters
Who have sense enough to make
The latch from roses
And the door from reeds, so that
The lover may enter his sweetheart's house
At any hour;
With fine linen on the bed
And the beloved waiting.

What she actually said to me was:
"Excuse me, but this palace
            is for the *Governor's* son."

I

Come swiftly to your love,
As a royal messenger spurred on by the
Impatience of his master—that is, if
Royal messengers are to be believed.

Come swiftly,
The entire stable is at your disposal,
The chariot ready.

No headlong horses
—When you meet her—
Will match the stampede of your heart.

II

Come headlong
To your mistress' house
Like the pride of the king's stable,
Chosen from a thousand thoroughbreds,
Trained on special feed,
Who breaks into unrivalled gallop
At the mere mention of the word stirrup,

43

So that not even the head-trainer
(Who is a Hittite)
Can hold him in.
How well he knows her heart
Who must always be near him.

III

Come as the desert gazelle
Spurred on to zig-zag in nervous haste
Crossing and re-crossing the track
In terror of yelping dogs and hunter;
Who at last has bearings,
And breaks off in a line of straight speed
With eye on the hideout.

You safe within your mistress' house
Kissing her hands, making
A fitting proclamation of your love,
You do all this
All within the great pre-destined framework
Of the golden goddess.